MY *Riteful* PASSAGE

MY *Riteful* PASSAGE

A Journey Through Life with God's Grace and Mercy

SUSAN LITTLETON-WILLIAMS

Final Step publishing

Suffolk, VA

My Riteful Passage: Journey Through Life with God's Grace and Mercy

Final Step Publishing, LLC
PO Box 1441
Suffolk, VA 23439
www.finalsteppublisher.com

Paperback ISBN: 979-8-9850005-6-6
E-Book ISBN: 979-8-9850005-7-3

Cover design by Cooke Classic Branding & Design | www.cookeclassic.com

For Worldwide Distribution. Printed in U.S.A.

Dedication

I dedicate this book to my daughters,
Maria, Monique, and Maya.

Mom always wanted you to know that you have your own story and your own voice. Please share your story with the world; you never know who needs to hear it!

Contents

Growing Up In Detroit

I was the eighth of nine children born to Julious and Mary Littleton in Detroit, Michigan, on April 26, 1962. Growing up with a large family was lots of fun and there was never a dull moment. There were seven girls and two boys—you can only imagine the conversations in the household. My older siblings treated me like a baby since I was second to the youngest. I grew up learning a lot about the generation in the '60s since some of my siblings were sixteen years older than me.

I recall when my oldest brother came home from Vietnam. Everyone was excited, but I didn't really know who he was because I was so young when he went to war. So when he returned, all I saw was this tall man come into the house and hug my mother. My Mother was so thrilled, and this was confusing to me because I knew he wasn't my father. All I remembered about my brother was his voice because we had tapes of him talking to us, and he called me by my nickname, Polly. He looked at me standing in the kitchen after greeting my mother and said hi to me. I recognized that voice, and that's when I realized he is my older brother. I grew up on Pasadena Street, and there were approximately eleven girls and ten boys of the same age living in the neighborhood. With so many of us on the same block, there was much for us to do, and we didn't have to venture off to have fun. We would play jacks, jump rope, hopscotch, hide and seek, running games, and card games such as Spades and Bid Whist. Bid Whist required you to be competitive in order to keep playing. If you and your partner didn't win the bid, then you would have to get up from the table, and you never knew when you would sit down again. I got my card skills from my parents and older siblings, who were great card players. My family would play cards at our family reunions every summer, and this was competitive as well. If an older relative chose you as a card partner, this meant you had proven yourself as a good Bid Whist player. We had fun laughing and trash talking about achieving the ultimate win by running a Boston on the other team. Running a Boston meant your team would win all the books and win the game. In the winter when it snowed, we would have snowball fights and sled rides. We had so much fun and learned a lot about forming relationships and getting along with others.

I remember going to the movies with my older sisters and their kids. Because of the age difference, my sisters had kids when I was four years old, so I grew up with my nieces and nephews. Imagine that: being four years old and an aunt! We would go to the Eastern Market with my dad. He usually took me, my brother who was one year older than me, my sister who was one year younger than me, and our four nieces. When we walked around the Eastern Market with my dad, people couldn't figure out if he was dad to all of us, or were some his grandchildren. People were astonished when they found out my dad was our father and my nieces' grandfather. One time we walked around, there was a politician campaigning for the Mayor of Detroit. He saw us and wanted to talk with my dad and get a picture with all of us.

I really remember that because I thought that was so cool to take a picture with a politician. We always had these types of experiences because my dad would take us to go to the park, swimming, and do various activities to give Mom a break. Those days were so fun, and times were so innocent.

I would say that I had a normal childhood, but as we grew older, we started experimenting with drinking alcohol, smoking cigarettes, and eventually, smoking marijuana. We weren't old enough to purchase any of these items, but they were always available in our homes. I believe all our parents smoked cigarettes during the '70s and we could sneak cigarettes without them realizing. Some of my friends would buy a pack of cigarettes and we would share with each other. We would get a cup of some alcohol whenever there was a party happening. We couldn't get a lot of alcohol on our own, so we would share with whomever could get something to drink periodically. As for marijuana, we started smoking in high school. Different people we knew in the neighborhood sold this, so it wasn't hard to get at all. By the time we entered high school, drinking and smoking were the norm. Thankfully, our parents weren't aware of this, and we didn't have any issues with addiction. All the neighborhood children grew up to be decent citizens, with none of us going to prison, dying prematurely, or becoming addicts. Despite our behavior, we had the fear of God in us. We all loved the Lord.

While in high school, several of the girls from our block started a club. We wanted to have a club similar to a sorority, where there would be a structure like an organization, and we would have functions similar to college sororities. We gave ourselves the name "Ladies of Unique." We had a symbol for our club and got our name and symbol trademarked, so no other organization could use our name or symbol. We were all very popular in our high schools, so anytime we advertised we were having a party, our function would sell out and it was the talk of Detroit. We made a lot of money, having parties and selling candy. Our only problem was we didn't have trustworthy people handling the money. The club broke up because our treasurer stole or misused our money from the last function. It was really sad because we enjoyed coming together and having functions, but when we started inviting people who didn't live on Pasadena Street, things didn't go well. We dissolved the club, and that was the end of the "Ladies of Unique."

After graduating from Central High School, I attended Wayne State University in 1980. I lived at home instead of staying on campus. As a freshman, I met an older guy through one of my close girlfriends who was dating his brother. Now, I had boyfriends while in high school, but they weren't serious, and I remained a virgin. This guy was five years older than me. I started dating him without my parents' knowledge. Unfortunately, the more we dated and spent time together, the worse my behavior was. I was drinking and smoking marijuana a great deal and hanging out with his friends—this was definitely the wrong crowd of people to associate with. I started staying out late. My parents noticed a change in me, but they were trying to give me some freedom since I was in college.

During this time, my father was hospitalized for a surgery—and I'm ashamed to admit this—but I started taking advantage of my mother, who was not the disciplinarian. My mother was so kind and loving, and she wanted nothing but the best for my siblings and me. She allowed me more freedom to come and go as I pleased. I was really getting out of control. My mother was worried that something might have happened to me because I wouldn't come home often. I wasn't being considerate by at least calling her to let her know I was fine and would be home in the morning. I knew my mom would want me to come home right away, and I didn't want to because I was having fun. I must admit, I was really acting dumb and disrespectful. This would not have happened if my father was home; he did not tolerate disrespect. After surgery, my dad went to a rehabilitation facility. He was away from the home for the summer and into the fall before he returned. Once they discharged him from rehab, he realized how disrespectful I had become. I guess I was more than just testing the waters, because one day I went out with my boyfriend and did not return home until the next afternoon. We had partied all night, and I was so tired. My father was livid! He took the car keys from me and forbade me from using the home phone. (There were no mobile phones then.) I was so sleepy, I didn't even argue. I just went to my room and slept most of the day.

When I woke up, my father reiterated that I could not use the phone. *No problem!* So, I went down the street and used the pay phone to call my boyfriend. I told him I was being treated like a prisoner. He suggested I come live with him and his mother. There, they would treat me like an adult. On Monday after school, I went home to get my clothes and other belongings so I could move in with my boyfriend. My father was so upset he wouldn't even look at me. My mother was angry as well, but she expressed that although I hurt her, she still loved me.

Moving Out

Now that I was living with my boyfriend, I was partying, drinking, and smoking even more. I would go to school during the day and party in the evening. Even during this, God was speaking in my ear. I had established my spiritual walk from going to church with my family and the neighborhood kids while growing up. I was baptized at sixteen years old at my childhood church. So, I had a firm foundation with God.

Ironically, the church was in the same neighborhood where my boyfriend lived. I would walk past the church regularly, and I started feeling guilty about my behavior. To make matters worse, my boyfriend became physically abusive, and it got worse over time. He became possessive and would leave me at the house for hours and go off to do who knows what. One day, some neighbors that I was friends with asked me if I wanted to go play cards. I had finished all my homework and was just sitting at the house bored. We got back home late that evening and my boyfriend was already back and upset with me because I left the house to hang out with friends. He hit and slapped me as soon as I entered the house. I balled up in the fetal position, screaming as he hit my back. His mother eventually told him to stop. I knew that night I was done with this. I had never witnessed domestic violence in my home. Surely I wasn't getting ready to live this life. I had had enough and called my mother.

"Hi, Mama."

"Hi, Sue. How are you doing?

"Not too good."

"Oh, you don't enjoy living in the streets?"

"No, Mama. He is hitting me!" I exclaimed.

"Get your stuff together. I'm sending your brother to come pick you up."

I moved back home immediately and was safe in my parents' home. My return home felt like the prodigal son. My parents were so happy to have me back, and I was glad as well. This was an awfully humbling lesson for me: no matter how much they say they love you, no one loves you more than your family.

From this domestic violence experience, I learned a lot about how women can be manipulated and confused about certain emotions and feelings. I forgave him, unaware of how abusers target young and vulnerable women. I grew up sheltered under a strict parental household. I soon learned what my parents were protecting me from once I got in the streets, living with people who didn't have the same upbringing as me. It still took time for me to realize I needed to leave that type of environment. I had parents that still loved me and would accept me back home no matter how disappointed they were in me leaving. Thank God he gave me the nudge to put my pride to the side and call my mom so I could go home to my protected environment.

I realized I was looking for love in all the wrong places. I decided I needed to get my life back on the right track and focus on my education and building my relationship with the Lord. My mind was clear, and my focus was renewed. Since the enemy's plan with my boyfriend didn't work, he launched a new attack on my life and purpose.

The Encounter

3

I truly was back on the right track. I stopped drinking and smoking marijuana, and knew the best thing to help would be detoxing. As I continued getting clean, I started experiencing some strange happenings while sleeping at night. While in a deep sleep one night, I was trying to wake up, but felt like something was holding me down. I know I was awake. My eyes were open, but I couldn't move or say anything. I felt like I was paralyzed. I started to panic and scream in my mind, *Jesus! Jesus! Jesus!* when I noticed a light in the corner of my room. After I called Jesus's name in my mind, the heaviness that was holding me down stopped. I believe this was the evil fleeing because I called on the name of Jesus.   When I looked more closely at the light, it appeared to be an image of Jesus. Jesus showed himself to me and reassured me he was there with me. I witnessed his protection. The Word of God says that you can call on the name of Jesus, and the enemy must flee. From this encounter, I knew with no doubt that Jesus is real, and he lives!

This totally changed my relationship with God; it showed me how to walk by faith and not by sight. My encounter just made Jesus more real to me. It was as if the Lord was showing me who he was in image form, like his proof to doubting Thomas with the nail prints in his hands. He reassured me that I could always rely on him, even in tough times. My spirit was awakened. I started praying and studying the Bible more to get a better understanding. I wanted a more intimate relationship with the Lord. I wanted to be sold out to God and totally surrender to him. I sought him in everything and every decision. I began to fully rely on him and place all my trust in him and not things of this world.

Back on track with my relationship with God and earning my college degree, I still struggled. I knew I needed to stay faithful to the word and keep my focus pure and holy. However, I was still vulnerable to my flesh and my desire to have relationships with men. I wrestled with promiscuity. I was still searching and coming up with the wrong results. Although I wasn't connecting with abusers, I was connecting with womanizers and men who knew how to be sneaky and cheat. Who knew I would become a cheater as well? I believe we all were cycling through life and not committing to any long-term relationships. It just seemed to be that way in Detroit in the 1980s. We didn't want to get serious with anyone but were content having very short-term relationships and affairs depending on who made you feel good at the time. As the saying goes: hindsight is 20/20. I didn't see it that way while involved in it, but looking back, we were playing Russian roulette. Thank goodness HIV/AIDS wasn't as prevalent then because we may have dodged a bullet.

Falling In Love

I was sitting in the Student Center having lunch with some friends when I met the man who would be my real, true love. He caught my attention at a pure time in my life. Building my relationship with God was paramount, besides focusing on my studies. Plus, I was still trying to find myself. I was only nineteen years old, approaching twenty soon. He seemed like he would be the one, but you can never let your guard down. The enemy stands ready to always attack.

Nevertheless, I accepted the offer to go on a date. We started dating; I met his family, and he met mine. It really appeared like this could manifest into a lasting relationship. He really caught my attention fast with his wit and charm. There was something very intriguing about him and this was rare for me, as no one could really impress me per se. He was a lot of fun and very smart. He was the reason I changed my major in my third year of college right around the pivotal time of making that important decision of electing a major. I changed my major from social work—which I wanted to do and follow in the steps of one of my sisters—to business. When he talked with me about his major in accounting under the school of business, I ask him to tell me more. As he continued to speak about the importance of an accountant at a big corporation, that impressed and interested me much more than being a social worker or counselor. I changed majors right away. This set me back somewhat, but I wanted to spend as much time as possible with the man I loved.

Because I dated the wrong men for so long, I really thought this man would be my husband. We became exclusive. Although I often thought about my spiritual encounter with God, I became sexually involved and slipped back into my old ways. Still, this recollection did not stop me from staying in the relationship and remaining intimate.

About one year later, we started making plans to get married and start our own accounting business. However, it was also around this time that I started noticing some significant changes in "the man of my dreams." The time we normally spent together began to diminish. He seemed to go missing sometimes when we would regularly be together. I wasn't working, but he was, and he would consistently give me money to put in savings for our future. That stopped as well, so I knew something was not right.

My woman's intuition kicked in, and I knew there must be another woman in the picture, although he hadn't mentioned anything and still appeared as if we were exclusive. Soon enough, the truth came out. I was constantly pressuring him, and he finally confessed that he had a drug habit and was smoking crack! He also confessed to cheating on me with another woman that smoked crack with him. I ended the relationship.

It seemed like my heart was broken beyond repair. I was crushed. I truly believed we had a future together. He had taken advantage of my trust and now I felt I was damaged goods. However, I learned timely lessons: allow no one to pull me away from my relationship with the Lord, and to not give my heart so freely without guarding it.

Putting this into practice would be harder than I imagined. I kept going in the wrong direction with relationships as I became more and more promiscuous, dating several men. But I was sure not to let my heart get involved. I was flippant and didn't take into consideration how I was hurting others. I wasn't aware of the concept "hurt people hurt people."

One night, I was partying with some friends and they invited me to a cabaret. A cabaret is a function where you bring your own alcoholic beverages and the host has setups, such as cups, ice, pop/soda, food, and snacks for purchase. Some of my college friends gave the party, and my ex-boyfriend and his current girlfriend were there. However, when I arrived, there was a very handsome gentleman at the door as we entered the party hall. I looked at him and he smiled when he saw us enter. The excitement of the party distracted me, and I didn't pay much attention to him.

I was there to have fun. We danced, laughed, and drank the night away. Even though my ex-boyfriend was with his girlfriend, he still tried to garner my attention, but I was not interested. As this party ended, there was talk of an afterparty at some guy's home. We weren't ready to turn in for the night, so we attended. When we arrived, I spotted the same guy who was at the door at the cabaret. He was still smiling. He had asked for a dance at the cabaret, but we never got around to it. I did not want to miss the opportunity this time, so I said to him, "Let's dance."

We were dancing to a slow jam, and he whispered in my ear that he had been waiting for me for three years. I pulled away from him because I was confused. *How could he wait for someone he didn't know?* He told me he had always been attracted to me and had secretly watched me for years when I was in my previous relationship. He pulled me close and kissed me on my neck, telling me he had always wanted to do that. I again pulled back, shock at his bold move. We continued talking, and he expressed that if he ever had the opportunity, he would take his chance. He was very tall, about 6'3" or 6'4" and dressed very well. He groomed himself nicely and was very well mannered. I could tell he was raised well, since his appearance was totally Gentleman's Quarterly (GQ), and he had a marvelous smile. Although I had my guard up, he seemed to speak with me in a manner I could trust and feel comfortable with. He didn't rush me, but gave me the time and space to recognize his attraction and affection for me. We became a couple soon after, and our relationship got serious.

Dating to Marriage

We started getting more serious and spending much more time together. Since he lived near my college, we agreed I should move in with him to make my commute more convenient. Of course, my mom was not happy again. She kept insisting that we should marry. We had only known each other for six months and things appeared to be moving really fast. I was ready to leave my parents' home again, but this time I wanted to do it the right way. So, shortly after moving in, we eloped in Ohio; just the two of us. We were married by the Justice of the Peace. The reason we went to Ohio was because there was no blood test requirement as required in Michigan, and we could get a marriage license right away. The blood test was required in Michigan to make sure the people getting married didn't have sickle cell disease or the trait. I was not so much in favor of getting married immediately, but between him and my mother, they convinced me to give it a try. While married, I continued my studies at Wayne State University, and graduated with my bachelor's degree. I still hadn't healed from my previous relationship, which prevented me from giving my whole heart to my husband, the one that truly loved me. The previous relationship with the crackhead had a major impact on how I would treat other men in my life. I was determined to allow no one to hurt me like that again. So, I went into relationships guarding my heart at all costs, which is not beneficial or fair to any other relationship.

With a broken heart, I shouldn't have gotten into another serious relationship, much less get married. I married him because I was being selfish and I didn't want to be alone, knowing that he really loved me and wanted to please me anyway he could.

I believe I went into marriage with a cheating mindset. If you hurt me, I was going to hurt you. I started stepping out on my husband. Because I was being unfaithful, this caused me to suspect that he was being unfaithful too. And he was, and I would find evidence left behind in the car that we shared. A woman left lipstick-stained cigarettes in the ashtray and Kleenex on the car floor to signal her presence to me. I didn't wear lipstick, and when I questioned my husband, he would always look dumbfounded. He suspected me of cheating, so he cheated as well. We separated. Our immaturity led to neglecting the sacredness of marriage and the effort needed to make it successful.

My husband helped me move into my own apartment. He didn't want me to move out, but he recognized we were having serious problems. Our problems stemmed from a lack of communication and maturity, and perhaps separation would help us both determine whether the marriage should continue.

Instead of focusing on how we could improve our marriage, I started dating other men as if I wasn't still married. My husband became suspicious and started stalking me. He would watch the traffic going in and out of the apartment complex. I was working at a hotel during the night shift and needed transportation to and from my job since he had kept the car. I was dating a few guys and would be seen regularly with them taking me to and from work and out on dates to dinner, the movies, and the club. I was just enjoying my life and the freedom that came with it, not allowing myself to get serious because I was still married, after all. My husband was also dating, but he was only dating one woman.

When I would tire of the single life and dating random men, I would call my husband. Every time, he would come over immediately. We tried dating one another to rekindle our marriage, and it appeared to be working. Whenever I would call him, he would end all outside relationships, hoping to win me back.

I grew tired of this back-and-forth behavior and also grew tired of working the night shift at the hotel. So, I quit. My husband asked about my apartment payment. He got upset when I said other men were willing to take care of me.

One early morning in February 1986, the Lord awakened me, giving me instructions to go see the Air Force recruiter. I told my husband I needed to use the car to go see the Air Force recruiter. He was a little confused, but he brought the car over to my apartment.

Once there, I informed the recruiter that I have a bachelor's degree in accounting. He had me take the entry test to determine what career fields I would qualify for. I scored so well and had several options. I chose the field of logistics specialist. This was the closest field to one in business. The recruiter allowed me to enlist on a deferment, so I wouldn't need to leave home right away. This gave me time to get all my affairs in order with my husband and family. So, I wouldn't leave for basic training until June 1986.

When I arrived back home, I told my husband all that had happened. I told him that after I finished basic training, we could leave Detroit and start a better life for ourselves. He wasn't too happy, but couldn't deny that this was a good choice, especially since I had a hard time finding a good job in my field in Detroit. I knew this was a calling and God was placing me on the right path.

Next, I needed to speak to my parents. I knew my father would be happy because he had served in the Army, but my mother didn't want me to leave. My mother wasn't happy because she believed that all the women in the military were homosexual. I explained to my mother that was a myth. My father was elated because he knew the military provided structure and discipline, and he believed I was lacking in these areas. He thought my life in Detroit was heading towards a destructive future.

I had four to five months to pay off any debts and say goodbye to my friends and loved ones. I wanted to leave Detroit with a clean slate, so I moved back home with my parents. It was there that I started dating other men. There was one gentleman I met at a party and started dating. He was a really nice guy. We spent much time together going to restaurants and clubs. He would wine and dine me every chance he got, since he knew I would leave Detroit soon. I loved the attention he gave me and how well he treated me.

But life became a little complicated when my husband decided he wanted me back only. He was previously dating another woman, and I was okay with that because there was a new man in my life. My husband came to my temporary job at a printing company. His visit was unexpected, because I had plans after work to go out with the man I was dating. My husband's friend gave him a ride back home after he brought me his vehicle at work for my ride home. He knew someone was giving me a ride home, so his actions were just to get the pot stirring. However, I took the car keys to not make a scene at my job.

When my gentleman friend arrived and saw my husband's car parked in front of the building, he was confused. He wanted to know why his car was there, and I told him my husband dropped it off so I could drive myself home. My friend was so upset that he just sped off because he knew my husband's motive was to shorten the time I would have to spend with him. I got in my husband's car and followed him. I spent a few hours at my friend's house discussing why my husband left the car, hoping to convince me to return home instead of having dinner with my friend. We both knew my time was running out before I was to depart Michigan and we wanted to spend as much time together as possible. He felt like my husband and I would get back together, so he was trying to take as much of my time away from my husband as possible.

I drove home after that, and when I arrived, my dad told me that my husband had called several times. I returned his call and told him to come pick up his car. When he arrived at my parents' home, I let him have it! He knew I was dating another guy, and even though he said he wanted us to get back together exclusively, he was still dating the other woman! This other woman got my phone number from my husband and called me. She even exclaimed that she was happy that I was going to the Air Force so that she could have him back. I wished her all the best.

My husband started crying and begging for my forgiveness. He also claimed that he hadn't told the other woman anything, so he doesn't know how she attained that information. He tried to make me feel guilty for not giving our marriage another chance and even said that he couldn't go on without me. I gave in and ended the relationship with the gentleman so my husband and I could work on our marriage 100 percent.

All was well from April 1986 through June 1986. In June, I left for basic training in San Antonio, Texas. From there, I went to Denver, Colorado, in August 1986, for technical training. Once I finished that, they assigned me to Lowry Air Force Base in Denver, Colorado. Before going to that assignment, I returned home to Detroit.

I arrived home wearing my Air Force uniform, which gave me a sense of patriotism. When my parents saw me in my uniform, they both were incredibly proud of my accomplishment. When I connected with my husband, I learned he was still cheating on me with the same woman. This woman called while I was at home. I wasn't concerned, but I was angry that she was bold enough to call the house. I was still the wife, and my husband was moving with me to Denver. I knew we needed marriage counseling to learn how to move forward and repair a damaged marriage, but I was still too immature to make this decision.

Air Force Bound to Denver, CO

My husband and I began our journey to Denver, Colorado. All we brought with us were our clothes, because we decided we needed a fresh start. I had already found a condominium right near the base, which was perfect, since neither one of us was familiar with the area. We would buy new furniture once we got settled in. This was a major change for my husband because he had lived nowhere other than Detroit.

However, my husband didn't stay in Denver for long. I disrespected him, mentioned another guy I met at technical training, and treated him poorly when I found out he was cheating again. It was with the same woman he had cheated with previously before I left Detroit for the Air Force. My behavior made him leave Denver. This marriage simply was not working, so he moved back to Detroit.

I found myself alone stationed at the Air Force Base working in Logistics for Civil Engineering (LOGCES) with no family or friends in the area. But this became a turning point in my life. Now that I was alone, I realized I needed to take a hard look at my life and turn back to God and my relationship with the Lord. I had become separated from my walk with him by not reading my word regularly, attending church, or praying. Although I stopped talking to God, he was always there and had never left me.

I was a great Logistics Technician—so much so that I ranked up quickly. This is rare for a start in the military. But it meant great things for my military career. I worked in the Civil Engineering Supply Group organization, and most of my customers were military men. I was in a position of meeting several men who were coming into the office frequently. Based on observation from my supervisor, these men never came into LOGCES to get supplies until I started working in the office. My supervisor continued to make comments about all the traffic for supplies recently.

After being on assignment for one week, I met a man who came into the inner office, which was reserved for the personnel that worked in LOGCES. My co-worker was super excited to see this guy; he was rather popular on the base. I assumed this was my first time meeting him since he was on vacation when I first started. He introduced himself, and I realized I recognized him from the Airman's Club. He laughed and asked if he could make up for what happened at the Airman's Club by taking me to dinner.

While in technical training, I went out with several of my fellow Airmen. We were at the club drinking and dancing. I'd left my drink on the table while dancing. The time was getting close to closing, and the waitress cleared the table and poured my drink out. When I got back to the table from the dance floor, I asked my friends where my drink was, and that's when they said someone poured it out. I made a scene! The man standing in my office was security for the club, and he was in civilian clothes, so that's why I did not recognize him in uniform. The people at the club apologized and gave me a raincheck for a free drink the next time I was in the club. In my office, he gave me his phone number and then left. I didn't want to date then because I was still married to my husband, and the wounds from our separation were still fresh.

The next day, while out making deliveries on the base, I saw the same man. He approached me and again asked if he could take me out. I felt honored that he asked me again, so I accepted. I explained to him that I was married but separated and was planning to divorce my husband. His demeanor after telling him about my current relationship situation didn't appear to make him reluctant to ask me out. I hadn't started any action toward getting divorced; it was all talk then. He continued to pursue me, so it made me believe he felt confident that he would have a good chance of a serious relationship with me. We immediately started dating, and soon after, became exclusive. We dated from early 1987 and married in September 1990. My divorce was finalized in March 1987.

I separated from the Air Force in January 1990 after being denied Officer Training School because the Accounting Officer's career field was too full. I was blessed to obtain an accountant position with the federal government at the Air Force Accounting and Finance Center in Denver on Lowry Air Force Base.

Married Life to Husband #2

I was blessed with a high civilian position because I have both a bachelor's and master's degree. I attended Webster University in Denver from August 1987 through March 1989 and earned an MBA in information systems. My Department of Defense experience added to my asset tools.

I gave birth to our first daughter, Maria, on November 9, 1991. Maria was about one year old when my husband was deployed on a remote tour to Korea. We could not move with him, so this started a series of military separations for our family. Early in our marriage began with us becoming accustomed to being apart.

In late Summer 1993, they approved my husband for a trip home known as a mid-tour. We planned a trip to New Orleans so he could visit his mom. We had been to New Orleans for Christmas several years in a row, but this visit was special since he had been deployed overseas for almost a year. I was very fond of his family as he was fond of mine, and our mothers adored both of us. They considered us the ideal couple.

During the visit, his family planned a barbeque party for him. We were all enjoying ourselves. While at the party, our daughter, at only twenty-one months old, thought she could play with her older cousins, who were about three years old. They were playing a game of jumping off the porch. When Maria's turn came, she fell and was in a gross amount of pain. I was very upset and yelled at him and everyone else that wanted me to calm down. My husband was on the receiving end of the bulk of the yelling because he was supposed to be watching her. I felt my husband was being extremely irresponsible. We took her to the Emergency Room and an x-ray didn't show any breaks. We believed she was in pain because of how she fell. However, when we arrived back in Colorado, Maria wouldn't walk because she was still experiencing pain. My husband had to return to Korea, so it left me with having to carry our daughter until I could find out what was wrong.

I took Maria to the military hospital in Denver for further examination. It had been two weeks since she last walked on her own. Based on the x-ray, the doctors weren't sure what was going on, so they decided an MRI would be best. I was a little apprehensive about Maria being put under anesthesia for the procedure, but it needed to be done. The MRI determined that she had a hairline fracture of the femur bone in her left thigh. Maria required a full leg cast because of the location of the fracture. Since she was still wearing diapers, it was somewhat difficult to keep her as dry as possible. We had to keep the cast wrapped in plastic for six weeks. Caring for Maria and working full-time was arduous, but we got through it.

Soon after, I found out I was pregnant. All was going well over the next several weeks, with Maria healing and needing to be carried. I was pregnant and carrying Maria at the same time. I went back to the doctor, and we removed the cast after six weeks. This was October 1993, right before Maria's second birthday. Her femur bone had healed, and she was able to walk again.

Not long after, my husband returned from his assignment overseas and was stationed at a base in Sacramento, California. We decided it was best that I stay in Denver since I was stable and had a good job. I had recently been promoted to a GS-12, which was good for us. GS-12 isn't an easy grade to come by, so staying in Denver made the most sense.

My husband had come home to Denver for a visit. One day, we were at home watching TV, and I made us lunch. I was boiling hotdogs, and the pot with the boiling water tipped and splashed on my foot. Even though I had on socks, I burned my foot. The pain was excruciating, so my husband took me to the hospital. I had second-degree burns! I left the hospital with my foot wrapped and a boot on my foot. My co-workers were concerned about me. Because my husband was stationed in California and had returned to his duty station, I was alone with our daughter and pregnant. They didn't want anything to happen. I tried to be much more careful after this.

As my pregnancy progressed, doctors diagnosed me with an autoimmune disease called Idiopathic Thrombocytopenic Purpura (ITP) which caused my platelets to have lower levels. My OB-GYN explained that I would have to take a steroid as I neared delivery. This medication was to prevent me from hemorrhaging. My strong faith in the healing power of Jesus Christ took over! I constantly prayed, "Jesus, by your stripes, I am healed."

I wasn't really showing any signs of ITP and didn't want to take any medication during my pregnancy. My obstetrician continued to insist the closer I got to delivering my baby. I was going to the doctor's office every Friday. On Friday, April 8, 1994, I had an appointment. I had been praying about the health of the baby and whether I should take the

Prednisone to prevent any complications during labor and delivery. I received confirmation from God to take the medication. The same weekend, I developed an alternate plan in case my husband did not make it back to Denver in time. I had dinner with a friend to make sure someone knew what to do if I went into labor early. The baby wasn't due for another two weeks, but I prepared my friend to pick me up and take me to the hospital and pick up my daughter from her daycare provider.

I trusted God and knew all would be well. I took the first pill on Sunday, April 10, 1994, and was awakened early in the morning the next day with stomach pains. I tossed and turned, rubbing my stomach, and then questioned why the pain was consistent. I turned to look at the clock on the side table and realized the pain was happening every 15 minutes. It then dawned on me that I was in labor, and this was not ordinary stomach pains but contractions! I immediately rose and called my friend to let her know. I had to dress myself and my two-year-old daughter. My friend arrived and took us to the hospital. By the time we arrived, the contractions were closer together. I had been leaking fluid for over a week, but the doctor didn't think it was amniotic fluid. Indeed, it was, and there was none left in the sack. When the nurse checked me, I was fully dilated, and the baby's head was starting to crown.

I believed God had answered my prayers because I had only taken one Prednisone and was now in labor. I just continued to thank God for what he had done. I gave birth to another healthy baby girl. She looked so much like Maria. I now have two daughters, two and a half years apart.

My husband didn't make it home until a few days after the baby was born. The new baby brought us joy, but we had to decide what to do as he was stationed in Sacramento while the girls and I were in Denver. We had two options: He leaves the military with early separation and returns to Colorado or we move to California. The choice was hard because of the great government job I had. We really couldn't afford to give up my pay, so there would need to be a compromise. Also, we really couldn't afford to maintain two households; someone would need to move. I started praying to God and asked him to intervene on our behalf and show us what we should do.

Several months went by before we decided. I helped my husband apply for jobs in Colorado if he retired early. He had received a job offer, but he really didn't want to retire. He enjoyed his career in the military and felt that we could do better as a family with him remaining in the Air Force. The only other option was for me to find a job in Sacramento at my current grade level and pay. That would be hard to come by. The accountant positions at my grade level weren't prevalent on the military bases.

I continued to fast and pray, seeking God on a strategy to get a position in California where there were few openings. While praying and cleaning on a day off, the Lord told me to speak to the Director of DFAS-Denver (Defense Finance Accounting System-Denver). This was not an act someone would do under normal circumstances, especially at my pay grade level. After all, I was only a GS-12, and the Director was a Senior Executive. But I was going to follow God's lead. I believed that if God directed me, he would align the paths for it to happen.

On a Monday in July 1994, I scheduled a meeting to talk with the Director of DFAS-Denver. The Lord put it in my heart to be honest about my family situation. I was going to meet with the Director to discuss a potential accountant position at MacClellen Air Force Base in Sacramento. The Director was the authority in charge of Operating Locations (OPLOC) and could make a request for a position to transfer me to Sacramento. I knew the Lord would grant me favor with the Director. Of course, the meeting went very well. He gave the task of finding me a position to the Colonel in charge of OPLOCs. His statement to the Colonel was to get this done and get me assigned to MacClellan. They put the personnel request into HR to search for accountant positions meeting my grade level. Only one slot was requested. I knew the HR specialist that was working on the submitted request. Because this request was during the critical summer of 1994, where positions were being frozen because the DOD was taking budget cuts, the request processed through a special system that handled positions which were frozen from hiring. The government was under a freeze due to budget constraints. Nevertheless, the Lord was guiding me to show himself strong!

Once the request was approved and submitted to Human Resources, it had to go into a system which handled the entire Western Region from Colorado to California. Because of the government freeze, several people were in the system with higher placement priorities than me. My friend, the HR specialist, went into the system to perform the action, but there was a dilemma. My priority was two and there was a man in the system with a priority one. The HR specialist had to assign the position to priority one, which left me without a position in California. The HR specialist requested another fill action to get me placed while the system was open, but the manager in charge of requesting the action said he could only take one shot at it. She told him before she closed the system to call Mr. Nabil, the DFAS Director, and let him know. The Colonel refused to call Mr. Nabil, so there was nothing else my friend could do.

I was off work the day all of this occurred. A friend called and told me what happened. I was shocked. My husband had already prepared for me and the girls to join him. He was getting on-base housing set up. He had also arranged private home childcare for the girls, who were now three years old and four months. These arrangements were not easy and required a lot of coordinating. Now, I had to tell him we weren't coming because a priority placement took the slot. I couldn't just leave my job in Denver without having a job lined up in Sacramento. I was so angry about the entire ordeal that I knew I needed to seek God in prayer. While praying, the Lord placed it in my heart to set up another meeting with Mr. Nabil. As I prayed about the situation one weekend in August 1994, the Lord was revealing a strategy to me. I know it was truly God-inspired because I would have never thought of it.

This act of faith was really a very significant turning point in my life. God really showed up and showed out on my behalf. Every time I think about how this all worked out and knowing nothing like this had ever happened for anyone in the past, it just showed how faith in God and the power of believing can really manifest into blessings upon blessings. People who may have been skeptical in the past could start believing in the power of prayer and faith in God.

Miraculous Move to Sacramento, CA

The Lord gave me the miracle strategy to use in my meeting with Mr. Nabil. And it was effective! I could not keep this miracle to myself; I witnessed to several co-workers how the Lord had blessed my family and ordered our steps. Because I had been talking with several co-workers about the process, telling them how hard this would be because of the government freeze, none of them thought it would be possible. So, I could testify to the goodness of the Lord and how he was operating in my life. God moved and answered my prayers, even when it seemed like all was lost.

God told me to ask Mr. Nabil if there was a way to waive the stopper list requirements so they could place me in the other vacant position, since they had filled the first position by the priority one person on the list. The stopper list is an identifier of federal employees that have been laid off from federal service and need to be re-employed in a priority order. Mr. Nabil liked that I had come prepared with options and not just a problem with no solutions. The Holy Spirit revealed all this because I knew nothing about the HR hiring fill actions with a stopper list involved.

Mr. Nabil immediately contacted the HR Director to contact the Western Region Stopper List group to ask the question. It was determined that this was possible, and without delay, they immediately placed me in the position and received moving orders to Sacramento within two weeks.

I started running about the building shouting, "God moved!" to everyone. People were so astonished and shocked because they never saw a mighty move of God play out in anyone's life before. All I could do was thank God because he had been so good to me, never leaving or forsaking me.

I started scheduling the military move. In September 1994, my husband came home to help me drive to California. We drove our new Toyota Camry from Denver to Sacramento. We had Maria in her car seat in the front and I was in the back seat with our four-month-old infant Monique. Thinking back, that was not a smart or safe move. As my husband was driving, he took his eyes off the road for a split second to look at Maria. Suddenly, our car went off the road into some soft, muddy grass—almost like a ditch—and he turned the wheel in the opposite direction while going 65 mph. The car was spinning around on the highway in the wrong direction! My husband hollered, "Jesus!" and the car came to a stop without flipping.

After the car stopped, I immediately told him to turn us around and pull over to the side. Glory to God, there was not any oncoming traffic, so we could get to safety. We had no damage to the car, and we proceeded on the highway. Surely the Lord was traveling with us and kept us safe all the way to California.

Upon our arrival, the girls and I needed to get familiar with the area since this was new to us; my husband had been stationed there for seven months already. We had a meet-and-greet with the new in-home daycare provider, Ms. Pam Greene. The girls seemed to be comfortable with her right away. God was working out everything in our favor, and I was so grateful to God because leaving my babies with just anybody wasn't going to work.

I started my new position as a GS-510-12 Staff Accountant. After being apart for more than a year, I was so happy to have my family back together. I was told that no one has ever come into the organization the way I came in transferring from Denver. It was indeed a blessing to get this position during a government hiring freeze. It was nothing but the grace of God and him continuing to show me how he was operating on my behalf because I was sold out to him.

My position was fairly simple since I had been employed with the Department of Defense (DOD) for over eight years, with four of those years being in the Air Force from 1986 to 1990, and four years with the DFAS-Denver from 1990 to 1995. I had a wealth of knowledge in all areas of accounting and finance.

There were a few individuals in the organization that played a significant role in my positioning within the organization to achieve a level of management. One person who was very instrumental was Cecilia Bennett. Cecilia and I were not only co-workers, but we became close friends. I saw her as my mentor to move into management because she had more experience than me. She had held several management level positions and was very sharp. She trained me on the base level operations since most of my finance experience was at the headquarters level.

When I first came to the organization at McClellan Air Force Base, Cecilia was the chief of the stock fund branch. As we worked together, I became more knowledgeable in the flow of operations, which made me more valuable to the organization. My headquarters level experience became eye opening as we cleaned up negative accounts. I worked closely with the accounts control branch to reconcile the foreign military sales, which were large at McClellan. The base, a major supply depot, had numerous transactions to account for due to providing goods and services to foreign countries. I started working with the accountants in the branch and coordinating with headquarters.

While becoming more familiar with the base level operations, the girls were getting acclimated to being in California, the sunshine state. They enjoyed being able to play outside at home in the evenings, which was such a difference from being in Colorado. They were growing up and really experiencing a whole new life. Everything was working out well in California and I was eager to find us a new church home as soon as possible.

I started visiting churches in the area because I was still getting familiar and no one at the job seemed to attend church regularly. I attended a church that was predominantly white. The people were really nice, and the girls enjoyed the children's church. My husband didn't attend with us, so we just went by ourselves. He got upset when we went to church, like he was trying to control what we did as it pertained to worshipping. We still went anyway.

Now and then, we would get into an argument when I told him I and the girls were going to that church again. I invited him and asked him if there was another church he wanted to attend, but he had no suggestions, so we kept going to the same church. Eventually, I found another church that was more predominantly African American, although it was further away from the base where we lived. My husband chose not to attend this church either. I just left it alone because he really didn't seem to care about going to church with us. I kept telling him we needed to worship together as a family, and that the only reason we could move to California was because God made a way. We needed to worship God together to keep our family blessed and covered under the blessings.

Career Change to Management

Since I had worked in both supply and Foreign Military Sales (FMS), I had a great understanding of country, case, and management accounting. Those were the types of accounts that had the problems.

My experience put me in a position to interpret to the staff at McClellan what Headquarters needed to address which helped clear the negative account problems. This level of experience was so unique to the federal government because everyone doesn't get the opportunity to work in a department like FMS, which is the department that sells weapons, equipment, aircraft, tanks, and training to other countries. One of the major problems a lot of the bases were having was being able to reconcile this information to ensure the books and accounts for the funds were balanced. The organization was excited to have me onboard because of my knowledge. I could clear millions of dollars that had been out of balance for the accounts. I had a skill set that no one else on the base had. This put me in an excellent position to leverage my abilities and be promoted because of what I could do. Once I worked in the department with the other accountants to clear up the reconciliation problems, the Director wanted to place me in a management position to run the department.

It was an amazing feeling and so fulfilling that I

could assist with a major effort to restore millions of dollars requiring full reconciliation. I could execute all I had learned for good to help the organization; then they could see why I needed to come to their base. I could make a difference and bridge the gap between headquarters and base level, so we could all work together for the greater good. I did not realize it at the time that God was setting me up to step into the Accounts Control Chief position. The current Accounts Control Chief left the organization after being offered a position with Hewlett Packard shortly after I assisted the branch with the negative accounts clean up.

Once she departed, I had a conversation with the director to inform him of my experience and the help I provided to close out millions of dollars in negative accounts. The leadership team transferred me from the Staff Account position to the Accounts Control Chief position. This move marked the beginning of my career in management and supervision in the Federal Government.

Shortly after assigning me to the Chief position, I needed supervisory training and was sent to Maxwell Air Force Base in Birmingham, Alabama, for Accounting Officer Training in Financial Management. I was apprehensive about leaving my babies for six weeks to get the training, but I knew it was necessary for me to excel in my career. All the Chiefs I had spoken to had attended the same training, and it was essential for me to be trained to continue to move in the direction the Lord was leading me in.

Attending this training placed me in circles to network with upper-level professionals in higher grades than I was in. I started growing my professional network with people of various levels in the Accounting and Finance community in the DOD. Making these connections was allowing me to expand my network. This helped me increase my net worth by getting promotions because I was being exposed to information that I would not have known if I just sat behind a desk doing the same job.

I loved Birmingham. The city was beautiful. I loved the old-style homes and all the trees and beautiful landscapes. Coming from Colorado and California, where the terrain was mostly dry desert with rock beds and palm trees, the south was a more beautiful nature environment. This training was for grade levels GS-12, 13, 14, and military officers, majors, and colonels. It was considered a high-level training, and I built extensive networks meeting people in the industry from all over the world. I made several new valuable friends and colleagues during this training.

One friend that I have kept in contact with over the years is Glenda Medford. Glenda was originally from the West Indies and was living in Germany at the time we met. She and I shared a room while in Alabama. She, too, was very smart and shared a wealth of knowledge. I believe the training was so much smoother since she was there with me. The training enhanced and built my leadership skills to help me become a valuable supervisor and manager.

While in Alabama, my girls were growing up in California without me. I enjoyed our talks during the week so they could share all the exciting things going on in daycare. During this time away, I reflected on my life and matured into the woman God was forming me to be, while also considering the direction of my life. Spending time with other professionals in my career field gave me some more ideas about where I desired to go career wise. It was a great opportunity for me to receive this level of training and work on projects with other professionals to learn better time management and team-building skills. Although the training was great, and the area was excellent for good food and fun, I missed home and my family. However, after returning from training, I had to deal with the reality that my father was an alcoholic.

My Father: An Alcoholic

I was back home in Sacramento, asleep in my bed, when I was jolted awake at an early hour. This differed from anything that had happened to me before. It had to be around 4:00 a.m. or 5:00 a.m. when I woke up from a dream. In this dream, my father was yelling for help. This startled me to my soul, so I called home to find out was everything okay.

I spoke with my mom, and she informed me that my father had been drinking heavily that weekend. Previously, his doctor told him he needed to quit. The Lord laid on my heart to write a letter to my father—I had so much respect for him, and I felt like I would have disrespected him if I talked to him about his problem.

I wrote the letter before Father's Day June 1996 and sent it with his Father's Day card and gift. I wrote that I really loved him and wanted him to be well and saved from his sins. My dad read the letter and started calling me reverend. I just wanted my dad to receive salvation. I did not want him leaving this earth without acknowledging Jesus as his Lord and Savior.

My dad didn't stop drinking even when the doctor told him it was damaging his liver. My dad believed that the doctor didn't know what he was talking about. He had no intention of stopping drinking. I know that alcoholism is a disease and until the person wants to get better, there is nothing we can do to help them.

As a little girl, I always remembered my dad drinking beer and sometimes scotch. Until I really learned about alcoholism, I thought drinking until you were drunk was normal. He worked at a plant during the week, needing to be at work around 5:00 a.m. each morning, so he drank on the weekends. When I think about his patterns, my dad really was a functioning alcoholic. When he wasn't drinking, he was somewhat quiet, but when he was drunk, his voice was loud. I know he knew the Lord because he was raised by parents that were born again believers, but from what I can remember, he was not going to church. He would wake up on Sunday mornings, play gospel music, and sing praises to the Lord.

During the week, after arriving home from work, he would read the newspaper, eat dinner, watch the news, and maybe watch a TV show or sports game before heading to bed. On Fridays when he got paid, he would bring the money home to my mom and go drink beer with his buddies. The drinking would last all weekend, but he went to bed early on Sunday night to be rested for work on Monday. His drinking was heavy while he was off work or on vacation, but when he had to work, he would drink no more than two beers. He curbed his drinking to weekends while employed, but drank more often after retirement. He wouldn't drink like he did on the weekends because he took over baby-sitting duties for the grandkids during the day and needed to be attentive. Once the grandkids no longer required babysitting, his alcohol intake increased during the week.

The continued drinking was taking a toll on his liver and overall health, but this didn't stop him. I don't believe anyone in our family wanted to recognize our dad was an alcoholic. When I started thinking about other family members—uncles and aunts on my father's side—it appears it was a bigger problem than just my dad, but no one wanted to talk about it or recognize it.

Thanksgiving 1996, my family returned to Detroit. My dad drunk the entire holiday weekend. I was so sad; I cried in private when I saw what my dad was doing to himself because he was literally killing himself with alcohol. My family arrived back in Sacramento the Sunday after Thanksgiving and learned that my dad had a massive stroke. The stroke was dreadfully damaging and left him unable to walk; his brain function was limited as well. My father seemed to revert to an infant. He recognized us, but he wasn't in his right mind, and his quality of living was awfully diminished. He was confined to a hospital bed or wheelchair, wearing adult diapers for the rest of his life. He was in the hospital for several months. To take some of the pressure off my mom, my siblings and I got the house ready for him to come home and receive around-the-clock care until he transitioned.

Four of my sisters and two of my brothers helped our mom care for our dad in his bedridden state. I couldn't help but think that the alcohol binge he went on that Thanksgiving weekend caused the stroke. Sure, there were other factors—he had high cholesterol, was a cigarette smoker, and exercised little—and they all played a role. Aside from those things, he was in pretty good shape for a seventy-five-year-old man.

While caring for my dad when I would come to town, I would always pray for him and talk to him about Jesus. I was praying for his soul. I knew he wasn't in his right mind, but I felt like the Lord had him. God was giving me the reassurance that he had to put my dad down on his back because now he couldn't drink or smoke; he could only lie in the bed and sit in the wheelchair, so now he had no choice but to listen. It wouldn't be any more running or escape from aligning himself with what the Lord had for him. The Lord had eternal life for him, and the enemy couldn't entice him anymore with drinking and smoking.

One day, while Maria, Monique, and I were visiting New Year's Eve 1997, I was feeding my dad, and he looked up at me and said, "When are we going to the big feast?" My holy intuition and instinct was letting me know daddy would be okay. We could let him go now because he was ready to go to Glory. I told him real soon and said, "Jesus will let you know when." He repeated what I said, and I told him, "Yes." After that wonderful exchange, I felt like the Lord was giving me the reassurance that my dad was going to be okay and would go to Glory. I continued to thank the Lord and told God that I was ready for him to take my dad home to Glory, because he didn't deserve to live on earth with no true quality of life. Our family was trying to hold on to him, and that was selfish and unfair.

My father lived for a little more than a year after that stroke. My girls and I went back to Sacramento in January 1998, and we received the call the next month. He died on my sister Angie's birthday—February 9, 1998. I was assured my dad was going to heaven. I told my siblings about that last conversation I had with him and reassured them that Dad was in Glory now.

Dealing with the reality that my dad was at the end of his life was a hard fact to realize. I knew his condition wasn't turning around because of the brain damage from the major stroke. He wouldn't have his faculties to live a normal quality of life, and just having him in that state wasn't fair to him or my mom. It was as if my mom was in prison because she had to be there all the time. Daddy needed twenty-four-hour care. I just prayed that the Lord's will would be done. I didn't want my daddy to leave earth either, but I know that we all must live and die. This is everyone's order when we were born into the earth, and I knew Daddy's time was near. I believe I was the only child that really was dealing with this reality and knew that the time was near.

I am still thankful to this day God gave me the urging to go home for the new year holiday although we were in New Orleans for Christmas. My husband wasn't happy about this. I told him that the girls and I would bring the new year in with my parents because I didn't know how much more time my dad would have here on earth. I wanted my babies to see him, although they were too young to understand what was going on. Maria was four and Monique was two. He was their only grandfather because my husband's father had passed years earlier before they were born. It was important to me they knew the only living grandfather they had. I didn't disagree with my husband usually; I generally just went with the flow. But I had to put my foot down on this decision, and we left New Orleans a couple of days after Christmas to be in Detroit for New Year's Day.

11
Living Without Daddy

After the funeral was over and we all went back home to our residences, we worried about Mama being by herself. My oldest sister was living in Laurel, Maryland, at the time and she was getting ready to retire. She had separated from her husband and decided to move back to Detroit. It was settled that she would move into the house with Mama. That way, Mama wouldn't be alone, and they were both good company for each other. Mama was living life, going on trips to the mountains with her cousins and lady friends that she just visited with occasionally in the past. While Daddy was alive, she went nowhere unless she went with him. She lived her life totally for him. So, it was so refreshing to see my mother just live a little. We were so happy for her. Although we missed Daddy as much as Mama, it was nice to see her enjoy life.

I flew my mother out to California to visit with me and my family since she had never been there before. This was her first time flying, and she enjoyed the flight with how quickly the airplane can get you to your destination rather than driving in the car. She had only traveled in the car in the past, so this was definitely different, and she wouldn't be the same. She wanted to fly everywhere after that experience, and we did just that. I would take her on trips with me and my family to New Orleans and Las Vegas. She was really enjoying traveling with my family and me. She also flew out to Colorado when we moved back there. Mama enjoyed her trips with me because we would always go to the casinos. My husband and I would give her spending money, and she loved playing the slot machines. We had so much fun together. I really got to see another side of my mother that I hadn't seen before, and maybe that is because I wasn't grown up or just because she couldn't do a lot when my dad was alive. She enjoyed traveling from place to place. I would let her know when the next trip was, and she would have bags packed and be ready to go. I was so glad I could do this for my mom financially because she lived another ten years after Daddy passed, and she had so much fun before she transitioned. My husband and I were getting along pretty well, but now and then, we would have arguments over church and what activities we would put the girls in. He also liked to go out a lot with his friends, and I believe he started stepping outside of the marriage, but I didn't have evidence to support my suspicion.

I remember one visit when Mama came to Sacramento to visit. My husband took my car to go get him and the kids something to eat. Mama and I were going to a soul food restaurant for dinner to spend some time alone. The girls were on a sleeper sofa watching cartoons on the TV. I was in the back bedroom talking with Mama, and I noticed the girls were being unusually quiet.

I went to check on them, and pulled back the blanket, but only saw my oldest daughter. her sister was and she didn't know. I panicked because I knew she wasn't in the back room with Mama, and she wasn't in her bedroom. This was before cell phones, so I couldn't check in with my husband. I knew my two-year-old daughter had left the house. I told Mama she was missing and ran out the door. I looked down the block and saw some kids playing, so I started screaming her name and none of them responded that they had seen her.

Outside, I informed my neighbor that my baby was missing. She may have left the house as she didn't see my car, and could be searching for me by walking. My neighbor got on her bike and started riding toward the base gate she could have left out of. I went running in another direction, screaming her name, and all the neighbors were coming out to look for her as well. After about fifteen minutes, my neighbor rode back up with my two-year-old in tow. She said she had gotten pretty far up the street, but there were people sitting outside noticing she was walking alone. They didn't want to approach her and scare her, but they kept an eye on her. My daughter went outside and walked off the base down the street she knew I drove on. This was such a scary moment for me to know my two-year-old could have been picked up by anyone and taken away from us. Her Dad came back right after all the commotion had ended and she saw he was driving my car and not his own. I told him he just missed out on a heart attack moment—I had gotten all my exercise for the day running around base housing. This made me be so much more attentive and aware of little children because they can get away so fast, and there are so many crazy people out in the world. I truly thank God for his grace, mercy, and protection of our babies. God has always kept them. Even when they were in the womb, he was protecting them. I was pregnant with my two-year-old daughter when I had to deal with the blood disorder that would make my platelets drop to a level that could cause hemorrhaging. God blessed me to have this baby with no problems and with limited steroid medication, because I had just taken one pill and gave birth to her the next day. I knew God didn't send this miraculous baby to the earth for her life to be cut short or end drastically. Her being lost showed me how to be more observant and present in the lives of both my daughters. It also taught me how quickly things can transpire when we aren't presently cognizant of what is going on around us. The enemy is always lurking and trying to cause confusion, and the entire motive is to steal, kill, and destroy. I know the enemy wanted to take out my seed because the enemy knows God sent my babies here to the earth on assignment. As their mother, I would pray until my babies were old enough to pray and fight the evil attempts as well. My mom's visit wasn't as eventful after the episode of my baby being lost, but she did enjoy the rest of her trip to California. I had serious conversations with both my daughters after this happened because I never thought either of them would leave out of the house without an adult and being supervised. My two-year-old kept saying she was coming to look for me because she thought I needed her. She was acting as my protector, and I had to explain to her I could take care of myself. I continued by saying that she shouldn't do that again because there are bad people who may want to harm her. I had these conversations multiple times with them until they really understood the importance of being with a known adult before venturing outside.

12
Changes on the Base

We were continuing our lives in Sacramento, California, and traveling around the state from San Francisco to Los Angeles, showing the girls different things in California, from the vineyards to Disneyland and Sea World. There was so much to do in California, but because they were so young, what they could do was limited. But they had a lot of fun! Both girls really enjoyed the warm weather, and being able to play outside for extended periods of time was such a joy.

My work organization was reorganizing and was considering moving from Sacramento to San Bernardino, CA. I didn't want to move to Southern California, so I opted to move back to Denver, where I felt more comfortable raising our daughters. My husband wasn't too pleased with this as he couldn't move back because he was still in the Air Force and didn't have the flexibility to move as I did as a Federal Government Civilian. I washappy to move back because our marriage wasn't the best at this time, and I continued to ask my husband to go to marriage counseling with me because I wasn't happy. He continued to brush it off and do what he wanted to do—run the streets as he pleased. So, the responsibility of raising the children was on me.

He was abusive, more verbal than physical, but when we would get into a physical altercation, I was tempted to call the police. However, since I fought back, he would back off and apologize. He used the same excuse saying he was upset because I wasn't respecting him, and he promised he wouldn't do it again. I had already dealt with this in my previous relationships, and I wasn't planning to live my life walking around on eggshells. This move was my way of getting away and not revealing I was really leaving him, and not just moving for the job. I still had a couple of months before relocating, so I would bide my time and just deal with his verbal abuse occasionally.

I would insist he not speak to me disrespectfully around the girls, as I didn't want them to think this was okay. He would listen sometimes and other times he wouldn't. I would just be quiet to show him that you can't argue with someone if they aren't talking, hoping he would get the point. It was apparent he was dealing with issues and didn't know how to communicate properly without getting upset or cussing. I just didn't like dealing with a lot of confusion because I loved having peace. I wanted my girls to have a peaceful environment to grow and develop and not deal with a lot of arguing, fussing, and fighting. They didn't deserve to grow up in a toxic environment.

While preparing for the move, I needed to go to Denver for house hunting. Since my oldest daughter would start first grade, she would need to come with me so I could get her enrolled in school. We flew to Denver and got caught in a snowstorm. This was my daughter's first time seeing snow since we were in California for three years. We got stuck at her godmother's house, but had a really pleasant visit. I was sharing with my friend the struggles happening in my marriage, and she could relate because she had just gone through a similar situation. She could refer me to a divorce lawyer if it became necessary.

Once the snow cleared, we house hunted and found a place for us to live. After I finished arranging the apartment and got my daughter enrolled in school, I returned to California to get our house in order for our move. We were moving out of base housing and moving all our furniture back to Denver. This was a very stressful time for me and my husband, as he was upset we had to leave. I was excited on the inside to just get away from him for a while and get back to my church home that I had left when we moved to California. I really missed my church family and all my friends in Denver.

We continued to get the house prepared and argued occasionally over silly stuff. The stress of our family being separated again was getting the best of both of us. Our baby at the time was three-years-old, and she thought we were arguing, so she grabbed the toilet brush we used to clean the toilet to fight her daddy. We both looked at her trying to defend me, and we couldn't do anything but laugh. I said to him, "See how silly we look? Even the baby has better sense than us." We tried to stop arguing in front of the children, but that didn't last long. I had gotten familiar with this type of behavior, which was really sad and unhealthy. We had dysfunction in the relationship, and if things didn't change, the relationship would not last.

We scheduled the movers over the next couple of weeks and prepared to take the journey back to Denver, Colorado. We drove back to Colorado with our most prized possessions in the car and we shipped the rest of the household belongings on a large truck.

Move Back to Denver, Colorado

As we headed back to Colorado, the drive was uneventful, with only one little child instead of two. I had left our oldest daughter in Denver with her godmother since she had already started school. We stayed in a hotel at the halfway mark to not tire ourselves and made it back to Denver in two days. We couldn't wait to get there so we could see our oldest daughter.

My husband flew back to Sacramento after we were settled, and he felt that we were safe. After he left, I started thinking long and hard about divorcing him. I really had enough of all the arguing, and my woman's intuition knew that he was cheating. I felt he was going out too much with the guys in the military, and because I had previous experience with the military, I already knew people had affairs regularly. People being unfaithful was extremely common in the military, especially when the military spouse had to travel a lot.

The type of career field he was in had him traveling occasionally, and he would always return home acting differently. I felt he might be stepping outside the marriage, but I wasn't going to make a big deal out of it unless I saw it with my own eyes. He would always start an argument anytime he wanted to go out with the fellas. This was his way of leaving the home. Some former co-workers told me that when we lived in Denver the first time, people saw him at clubs talking to other women. I thanked my co-worker for looking out for my best interests, but if he was doing anything in the dark, it would eventually come to the light. I would confront him then.

My issue was that I would rather him just say he doesn't want to be married or faithful, and then we could part ways. But he never said that. He preferred to argue and sometimes get physical when I would fight back. I hated my daughters saw this type of behavior. I knew I needed to do something because I didn't want my daughters growing up in so much dysfunction.

I felt like since we were back in Denver and he was in California, I could start the proceedings. I went to speak with a lawyer and he told me that in Colorado, you must be domicile in the state for at least ninety days before you could file for a divorce. I continued to bite my tongue and not say anything.

Since we had only been in Denver for a couple of weeks and Thanksgiving was approaching, I decided we were going to stay in town for the holidays. I hadn't heard from my husband in a few days, so I didn't get the chance to tell him we would have dinner at a girlfriend's house. When I arrived back home, I saw that he had left several messages on the answering machine. After I put the girls down for bed, I began listening to the voicemails.

He was so angry. He was cussing me out and calling me many evil names. I shook my head and knew I needed to end this relationship because he was becoming more and more obsessed and belligerent. I knew I just needed to bide my time until the ninety days were up and then file for divorce. We eventually spoke, and I explained we were at a friend's house for Thanksgiving since we didn't go home to Detroit. He apologized, but the problem was he felt too comfortable saying such hurtful things and accusing me of cheating and being out with other men. I knew this is behavior someone has when they can't be trusted, so they accuse the spouse of doing the same thing. He sent two dozens of roses to my job to make up, but all this did was make a scene. The people at my new job were complimenting the beautiful gesture and believed I had a wonderful husband. Little did they know all that I was dealing with behind the scenes.

He called to ensure I received the roses, and this is when I told him the marriage was over. It shocked him because he thought buying roses and sending gifts would make up for what I had been feeling and experiencing for the past while in California. I suggested counseling several times to improve our marriage and set a good example for our daughters. He would always say that no one could tell him how to handle his marriage or be a father. He felt like we were fine.

When he heard me say I want a divorce, suddenly he wanted to listen to me. I didn't want to stay on the call with him while at work, because I had people in my office and I couldn't say what I needed to. I was at the end of my rope and wanted to throw in the towel. I couldn't continue to tolerate physical and emotional abuse. Also, he kept trying to pull me away from God, and that needed to end. Those behaviors are a definite no for me.

He was persistent on the phone, begging me not to do this and give him another chance to get it right. I told him I had given him so many chances and the last straw was he didn't want to get any counseling to help our broken marriage. I had to end the call, but said we could discuss this later when I got home. I had to hang up the phone on him because he wouldn't take no for an answer. I finished my workday with about three more hours of work, and then I left the office. I went to pick up the girls from school and daycare and we headed home.

Surpise Pop Up in Denver

After picking up the girls from school and daycare, we stopped to get something to eat. The girls wanted Happy Meals, and I grabbed a salad from McDonald's, and we headed home. Our normal routine once getting home is to eat, finish any homework, and take baths. The girls were very chatty this day, wanting to talk about their day and find out about mine. I told them I had heard from their daddy, and he had sent me lots of flowers. This made them really excited. They finished eating, and we looked over homework assignments that were due the next day. After the homework was done, it was time for baths and then a little television for entertainment before bedtime.

The girls were in their pajamas by 8:00 p.m. and I was also in mine, talking on the phone to a friend in California. She was warning me about my husband because she had dealt with a similar situation with her ex-husband, who was Air Force retired. She was telling me to be careful when you are dealing with possessive Air Force men, who don't understand how to accept no.

While talking, there was a knock at the door. I couldn't imagine who could be at my door, since many of the people we previously knew in Denver didn't know where I lived now. I had a couple of friends, but they didn't say they were coming by. When I looked out, I realized it was my husband. I was in shock and scared all at the same time. How did he get into town so quickly when I had just spoken with him earlier that day and he was still in California? The girls heard his voice outside the door and was begging me to let their dad in the apartment. I said, "No! I don't know why he is in town, and I am scared he may do something to me." They were too young to understand, so I ended the call with my friend. I called a friend that lived in Denver. I needed her to come over quickly since he was at the door and wasn't planning on leaving until he could talk with me. He kept saying, "God told me to come and save my family."

When my friend arrived at my apartment, she spoke with him for a few minutes and explained that I was scared because I told him I wanted a divorce. He promised her he would not do any harm to me or the girls; he just wanted to talk to me. My friend said that she would come in with him. I opened the door and let him in, and the girls were so happy to see their daddy. He hugged them and kissed them and then told them to go to bed while he spoke with me.

My friend went in the room with the girls, and I explained to him I was not happy in this marriage anymore. I begged him for counseling before we left California, but he resisted, so I just wanted out. He asked for another chance and could we seek counseling in Denver because he understands now that our marriage needs help and is in trouble. I told him I wasn't sure if I even wanted to try again because I was so tired of all the emotional trauma dealing with him. He promised to get help and do better if I gave him another chance. I told him I didn't know and I would need to pray about it and sleep on it. I also told him he couldn't stay here with me tonight. My friend offered to let him stay at her house with her and her husband. I thanked her and he hugged and kissed the girls before they left.

I couldn't believe this was happening. It seemed surreal. I called my friend from California back, and she, too, couldn't believe he left California that afternoon and was in Denver by the evening. We were both shaking our heads, thinking he wasn't going to give up. I went to bed shortly after I got off the phone with her, and I prayed before going to sleep. I asked God what he wanted me to do. I was so torn because I had dealt with this for over ten years and didn't feel like he was going to change. But the Lord softened my heart and opened me up to another chance at this marriage.

I made us an appointment with one of the marriage counselors/pastors at my church in Denver. Normally, you can't go to the church and get a counseling session the same day, but we did. I knew this was God orchestrated because it is usually not that easy. We met at the church and saw the pastor. He inquired why we were there, and I explained that my girls and I had recently moved back to Denver. I also explained that my husband and I had been married for almost ten years but had been together for about twelve years, if you include dating. I told him my husband was physically abusive at the start of our marriage. He ceased physical abuse after I threatened to leave, but resorted to emotional and verbal abuse. I was emotionally drained with this type of treatment and just wanted out.

The pastor asked my husband to explain his side of the story. He started sharing information I had never heard before, like how he never learned what a healthy marriage looked like and how to be loving and kind. He told the pastor he watched his mother try to take care of the family. They were poor, as his father died when he was a little boy, and his brothers had gone off to the Vietnam War. He talked about getting pails of water from the lake because they didn't have running water to flush toilets. He had gone through all sorts of stuff that I had never had to deal with as a child.

I was shocked hearing about the type of childhood trauma he was healing from. This made me feel some empathy for him and understand why he may not have known how to treat me. He needed help and compassion, so I gave our marriage another chance. I outlined deal breakers, including cussing, name-calling, and unfair treatment when disagreeing.

We started watching several marriage ministries videos from T. D. Jakes' ministry, in particular. My husband and I studied the word that dealt with marriage to better understand what God intended for a healthy, Christian marriage. We started going to church as a family in Denver because he stayed in town for one month, taking time off from his duty assignment in California. He explained he had a family emergency and his organization was very understanding. We continued working on our marriage, and it felt like we had gotten the passion back in our marriage, and we could be secure in giving this relationship another shot.

Once the month was up, he went back to California and started working on getting assigned to Denver. We spoke on the phone every day. He continued to make phone calls and talk with his commanders about a possible reassignment to Buckley Air Force Base, which was located down the street from where I lived. It only took a couple of months before God placed him to get reassigned to Buckley Air Force Base. We both knew this was nothing short of God's grace and favor over our lives, and it also gave me confirmation that God was working on our marriage. The girls and I were so happy when he got stationed in Denver, and we were all a family again. This worked out well for us because we needed to be in the same space as we were mending our relationship and trying to keep this marriage together. All I could say was to God be all the Glory for what he was doing in our lives.

Life was good, and I prayed that life would stay good, but I had seen this before. He started to inch his way back to his bad habits, like not going to church regularly and drinking a little more than usual. I just continued to pray and knew that God would work it all out. We weren't arguing, and he wasn't being verbally or emotionally abusive. But he was going to the club with his unmarried friends. Going to the club wasn't something I was interested in, so I allowed him to go without me. I've always felt like giving them enough rope to hang themselves, if that's what they chose to do. While he was out, I started something new. I started journaling the journey.

About the Author

Susan Littleton Williams is a passionate, self-motivated, take-charge type of woman. She has a wealth of knowledge and life experience and is considered a powerful influencer. Susan is a wife, mother, and grandmother that has reached several achievements and milestones in her life. She has a bachelor's degree in Accounting and a master's degree in Information Systems. Susan served the USA in the Air Force and retired after thirty-two years of Federal Service within various government departments. Susan has juggled several careers from the military, government, and now entrepreneur and employee-owner with an exceptional consulting company. She is a staunch believer that God has chosen her for such a time as this and wants everyone on earth to walk in purpose to fulfill their call to destiny. Born and raised on the Northwest side of Detroit, MI, she now lives in the Washington D.C./ Maryland/Virginia (DMV) area.